RAMONA QUIMBY

by
LEN JENKIN

From the novels of
BEVERLY CLEARY

Dramatic Publishing
Woodstock, Illinois • London, England • Melbourne, Australia

Adapted from the Ramona books by Beverly Cleary,
published by Morrow Junior Books, a division of William Morrow & Co.:
BEEZUS AND RAMONA ©1955; RAMONA THE PEST ©1968;
RAMONA AND HER FATHER ©1975, 1977;
RAMONA THE BRAVE ©1975;
RAMONA AND HER MOTHER ©1979;
RAMONA QUIMBY, AGE 8 ©1981; RAMONA FOREVER ©1984

Cover design by Susan Carle. Cover photo by Cheryl Walsh Bellville. *Used by permission.* The Children's Theatre Company of Minneapolis production, featuring (left to right) Megan Mostyn-Brown (Beezus), Christopher Bloch (Robert Quimby) and Emily Mostyn-Brown (Ramona).

ISBN 0-87129-330-7

RAMONA QUIMBY

A Full Length Play
For Five Males and Nine Females, Extras

CHARACTERS

RAMONA QUIMBY .... an imaginative, lively third-grader
who is sometimes wistful or sad

BEEZUS QUIMBY ...a conscientious older sister who loves,
but is often exasperated with, Ramona

DOROTHY QUIMBY ... a loving mother who is often tired

BOB QUIMBY . a father who is fun when he isn't down-hearted

AUNT BEA .... Dorothy Quimby's younger sister,
a third-grade teacher

HOWIE KEMP ..... serious third-grade friend of Ramona's

UNCLE HOBART .... Howie's rugged uncle
who works in oil fields, is full of fun, and likes to tease

MRS. KEMP .... .Howie's humorless grandmother
and Ramona's sitter

MRS. GRIGGS ...... strict third-grade teacher doing her job

SUSAN .. vain third-grader who doesn't like Ramona. Jealous.

TAMMY .... a high-school waitress

SELMA .... too chic saleswoman with stylish hair

MR. FROST .... large man with white beard

OLD MAN .... lonely man
wearing what are probably his son's old clothes

DOCTOR

DIRECTOR

Miscellaneous third-graders, wedding guests, Cub Scouts and
Brownies, Ramona's reflections in mirror.

WHAT PEOPLE ARE SAYING about *Ramona Quimby*...

"It was fun to work on a play for children that mostly avoided 'sweet' situations and resolutions. This play is wise and funny. It speaks to today's kids—and our audience loved it."
City of Davenport Parks Recreation, Davenport, Iowa

"Well loved by cast and audience alike! *Ramona* speaks to a variety of ages. Can't wait to produce *Henry and Ramona*!"
Darlene Lentz, Sand/Storybook Theater Center, Deland, Fla.

"Fast-paced, funny, yet poignant interpretation of the trials and triumphs of growing up, in addition to reinforcing family values in a society 'full of really crazy, scary stuff.' "
Jane Meier, Rundlett Middle School, Concord, N.H.

"This was, by far, our best-received production in our history. Just from word of mouth, our final performance was 'standing room only.' Since our entrances came from various parts of the entire auditorium, we had to literally step around and over people."
Scott Marcum, Oz Drama Group, Blockton, Iowa

RAMONA QUIMBY

*(Closed curtain. A yellow leaf falls in the light. Then an-
other. More leaves fly by. It's autumn.*

BEEZUS enters, jacket, jeans.)

BEEZUS. Hi. My name is Beatrice Quimby and my job is to
help you. Usually, at a play like this, or at the movies, we
see people really different from us: princesses, or detec-
tives, or presidents or even mermaids. Or people who lived
a long time ago, or even in the future. At school, you learn
a lot more about people really different from you, like a
unit on Eskimos where you study igloos and walruses and
blubber. So I thought, what about us? People like you see
in the street every day—or even like your own family. It
might be pretty neat if we took a good look close to home.
So my idea for this play, *Ramona Quimby,* is to take us all
to my house. Come on, I'll show you around.

*(BEEZUS opens the stage curtain, revealing Klickitat
Street.)*
Cross SL→SR following bike

BEEZUS. If you watch TV news, it looks like the whole
world is full of really crazy, scary stuff. Wars, and homeless people, and all—but the street we live on, Klickitat
Street, is just there, in a nice sort of quiet way. Sprinklers
and bikes and garage door openers, and the rows of houses

5

full of couples and their kids. A big bomb could drop on Washington, D.C., where the president is, and on Klickitat Street everybody would still mow their lawn. Sometimes I wonder what would happen if we didn't mow, but we always do.

SCENE TWO

(RAMONA QUIMBY enters. She looks over the street, BEEZUS, and the audience.)

BEEZUS. My mom says it looks nicer, and Dad says we wouldn't want our place to be an eyesore.

RAMONA. If we didn't cut the lawn there'd be a jungle— with armadillos and gila monsters and venus flytraps, and we'd get lost in it and never come out.

BEEZUS. That's my little sister Ramona. She exaggerates.

RAMONA. Ramona Geraldine Quimby. And her name is Beezus.

BEEZUS. Ramona! Let me explain…everybody calls me Beezus 'cause when she was a baby she couldn't say my name right. Beezus! Beezus! It stuck. She can be a pest sometimes.

RAMONA. If I am a pest, you are a rotten dinosaur egg.

BEEZUS. Let's ignore that, shall we.

(MRS. KEMP appears outside the Kemp house. She waters the flowers.)

BEEZUS. There's Howie's grandma, Mrs. Kemp. She lives next door with Howie. She used to baby-sit for me, and now if Mom's busy and I'm off at Pamela's or someplace, she baby-sits for Ramona. *(Calling over.)* Mrs. Kemp!

MRS. KEMP *(turns toward BEEZUS, spots the audience.).* Hello, Beezus. Who are all these people?

BEEZUS. Friends of mine.

RAMONA. Mine, too!

MRS. KEMP. Oh, hello, Ramona. Well, make sure they don't trample the lawn. *(Ad libs. MRS. KEMP heads off inside.)*

BEEZUS. She watches soap operas on TV. All day.

RAMONA. And her hair is getting thinner, too.

(An OLD MAN in a straw hat crosses the stage. He wears a slightly frayed dark suit, like an eccentric elderly academic.)

BEEZUS. Lots of other people live around here. Some of them are nice. *(OLD MAN looks curiously at BEEZUS and RAMONA as he crosses. Then he salutes energetically in their direction.)* Some are pretty weird.

(As OLD MAN salutes, a troop of marching CUB SCOUTS in uniforms sweeps past. A troop of BROWNIES, all holding boxes of cookies, enters opposite the CUB SCOUTS, crosses.)

CUB SCOUTS and BROWNIES.
    LEFT, LEFT, LEFT, RIGHT, LEFT;
    LEFT, LEFT, LEFT, RIGHT, LEFT;
    LEFT, LEFT, LEFT, RIGHT, LEFT;
    LEFT, LEFT, LEFT, RIGHT, LEFT;
    HAVE TO MARCH MY BIKE'S GOT A FLAT
    DOWN THE STREET CALLED KLICKITAT
    LEFT, LEFT, LEFT, RIGHT, LEFT;

LEFT, LEFT, LEFT, RIGHT, LEFT;
LEFT, LEFT, LEFT, RIGHT, LEFT;
WALKED ON A LAWN, GOT SPRAYED BY A HOSE
IN THE CITY OF THE ROSE
LEFT, LEFT, LEFT, RIGHT, LEFT;
LEFT, LEFT, LEFT, RIGHT, LEFT;
LEFT, LEFT, LEFT, RIGHT, LEFT.

CUB SCOUT LEADER. Corps, halt! Scout Law Formation! *(Whistle.)* Corps, ten hut!

BROWNIE LEADER. Scout Motto!

SCOUTS. BE PREPARED!

CUB SCOUT LEADER. Scout Law!

BROWNIE and CUB SCOUT LEADERS. Ready and...*(ALL SCOUTS do the Scout Law in sign language.)*

CUB SCOUT LEADER. Scouts...FALL OUT!

BEEZUS. And then some are just always around.

(As all SCOUTS march off, MR. QUIMBY enters, goes purposefully across the stage. He's wearing a winter hat with earflaps, and holds a heavy winter jacket.)

MR. QUIMBY. Beezus, don't forget to tell them about your sister.

BEEZUS. I did. I told 'em already. Here's my dad, Mr. Robert Quimby. *(MR. QUIMBY takes a bow.)* He's a pretty wonderful dad. He takes us all to fun places when the family budget can afford it. If you've got a school problem, you should ask him about it. He knows stuff about almost everything.

MR. QUIMBY *(modestly)*. Beezus, you're exaggerating.

BEEZUS. Am not. I am especially proud of my dad because he quit smoking two weeks ago, which was pretty tough to do.

MR. QUIMBY. It's still tough. And don't forget your Aunt Bea. Santa's helper is late for the North Pole. Have to run.

BEEZUS. That's a joke. My dad works in a frozen food warehouse. He'd like to be a teacher, but he can't right now. He's got to find time to go to college first.

RAMONA. He drives a fork-lift, whatever that is.

BEEZUS. As I was saying before all these interruptions, Klickitat Street is one of those places that's—well, sort of regular. And the next street over is pretty much like it, and the one after that, till you get to the highway.

RAMONA. Aunt Bea has a yellow convertible.

BEEZUS. It's really comfy here in a way I guess you could only understand if you...

RAMONA. Aunt Bea lives in the tallest building in the city.

BEEZUS. All right, Ramona. We'll introduce Aunt Bea, who lives in an apartment.

(In the distance, BEA appears in her apartment window. She is hip and fairly glamorous. Interesting music plays.)

BEEZUS. She's a third grade teacher. Ramona thinks she is the coolest person in the entire world.

RAMONA. Because she is. Aunt Bea has an apartment you get into with a buzzer. *(Pressing one finger onto the set somewhere. A loud buzzer sounds. BEA hears it, looks out her window, sees RAMONA and BEEZUS.)*

BEA. Who are those fantastic looking girls down there?

RAMONA. Ramona!

BEEZUS. And Beezus!

BEA. My own nieces! I thought so, but you both look so grownup I wasn't sure. What do you say we play hooky and go shopping for bubble bath and fabulous hats. *(RAMONA heads toward BEA, but BEEZUS grabs her and holds her back.)*

BEEZUS. Aunt Bea, you know we can't. It's the first day of school.

BEA. Neither can I, really, but it's a good idea. For another day. Have a fabulous first! Don't let it get boring! *(BEA laughs and disappears. The light in her apartment window goes out.)*

(HOWIE KEMP appears on Klickitat Street. He's carrying a package.)

HOWIE. RAMONA!

BEEZUS. It's Howie. Ramona's best friend, and our next door neighbor.

HOWIE. Hey, Ramona. Day one of third grade! We don't wanna be late.

BEEZUS *(looks at watch. To audience)*. I got to get to school myself. I'll tell you more later. It may look a little ordinary around here, but once you...

RAMONA. A car hit a telephone pole. You should tell about that.

BEEZUS *(trying to leave for school)*. Ramona, I'm trying to calmly introduce the neighborhood, so people can learn how we live here.

RAMONA. The telephone pole's in the neighborhood.

BEEZUS. Don't butt in, okay? *(BEEZUS exits. RAMONA shrugs, turns to HOWIE.)*

RAMONA. I wanna tease the second graders, like we got teased last year.

RAMONA and HOWIE. Second grade baby, stick your head in gravy, wash it out with bubble gum and send it to the navy!

(MRS. QUIMBY appears in front of her house.)

MRS. QUIMBY. Ramona, sweetie, you don't want to be late, and start off on entirely the wrong foot with Mrs. Griggs.

RAMONA. That's my mom. Her job is taking care of everyone. Me and Beezus, and my dad. She's very smart, and bakes amazing cookies that are better than anything except maybe Oreos. Or Ding-Dongs.

MRS. QUIMBY. Ramona! Off to school!

RAMONA. Mom, I'm talking to the audience.

MRS. QUIMBY. That's Beezus' job.

RAMONA. Why don't I get to...

MRS. QUIMBY. Because Beezus is older. Now go off to school.

HOWIE. Race you to the school yard!

RAMONA and HOWIE. Second grade baby, stick your head in gravy...*(RAMONA and HOWIE run off. Klickitat Street is gone.)*

EN USL

SCENE THREE

(A school yard fence appears. A sign reads: GLENWOOD SCHOOL.

SUSAN, with a beautiful head of curls, dressed for third grade success. She's carrying a package. HOWIE races on, followed by RAMONA.)

SUSAN. Hi, I'm Susan.

HOWIE. Hi, I'm Howie.

RAMONA. I'm Ramona.

SUSAN *(opens her glitzy shopping bag. She pulls out a gorgeous, curly-haired doll that looks exactly like herself).* This is Tiffany.

HOWIE. No kidding.

E✕ USR
E DS R   SCENE FOUR

(A bell rings. MRS. GRIGGS appears, along with the three desk/chairs of the classroom. RAMONA, HOWIE and SUSAN take seats, sit nervously at attention. MRS. GRIGGS is stern and domineering.)

MRS. GRIGGS. Good morning, class.

ALL. Good morning, Mrs. Griggs.

MRS. GRIGGS. Now class, in kindergarten we have cookies and juice, play "London Bridge," and have fun.

HOWIE. London bridge is fall...

RAMONA. Shhh...Howie.

MRS. GRIGGS. In second grade, we read about Dick and Jane, play dodgeball, and still have fun. You are now in third grade. Fun is not allowed in this classroom. We are here to learn. Any questions?

(As MRS. GRIGGS sternly strolls the class, BEEZUS appears in another area.)

BEEZUS. Oops! I forgot to tell Ramona. First day in Griggs' class is always Show and Tell. She sent a note to Mom in the mail, but that was the day Ramona turned all the letters into paper airplanes. Uh oh...*(BEEZUS is gone.)*

MRS. GRIGGS. I'm sure all of you are ready for Show and Tell.

ALL *(RAMONA with surprise and fear)*. Yes, Mrs. Griggs. *(RAMONA desperately considers everything within her reach as an object for Show and Tell—a hair clip, a dirty Kleenex, shoes. It's hopeless.)*

MRS. GRIGGS. Howie Kemp, what do you have for us?

HOWIE. My brick factory! *(He comes forward with his paper bag tied with twine. He unties it, takes a brick out, puts it on a desk.)* This is how I make bricks. *(He takes out a hammer, and smashes the brick to pieces. Brick dust and chips fly everywhere. He takes out another brick, lays it carefully where the first one was.)* Good work, men! Make more bricks! *(He raises his hammer again.)*

MRS. GRIGGS. That's quite enough bricks, Howie. Thank you for sharing. Susan? *(HOWIE sits, as SUSAN comes into the spotlight with her doll.)*

SUSAN. This is Tiffany. She has a beautiful new dress, and she's all ready to go shopping at the mall. First she'll go to Toys R Us, and then to Kandy Kitchen, and then...

MRS. GRIGGS. Thank you for sharing, Susan. Yours was an excellent example for Show and Tell. *(As SUSAN takes her seat...)*

RAMONA *(reaches into her pocket, takes out a small beat-up doll with blue hair)*. This is Chevrolet.

SUSAN. Nobody names a doll Chevrolet. That's dumb.

RAMONA. It's French. My Aunt Bea gave her to me, and she's named after my aunt's car.

SUSAN. What if your aunt drove a Mack truck? Would you name your doll Mack Truck?

HOWIE. I would.

RAMONA. No. But Chevrolet is the most beautiful name in the world. It sounds like a fairy tale name.

MRS. GRIGGS. Ramona Quimby! An overactive imagination leads to daydreaming, idleness, and wanting all sorts of things you can never have. Yours will get you in a lot of trouble in this class—someday. Class, open your readers to page 42. Today we're going to hear a lovely fairy tale. *Hansel and Gretel. (Reading.)* "Once upon a time, in a deep dark forest, lived a poor woodcutter and his children, Hansel and Gretel. One day... *(MRS. GRIGGS' voice fades under, as Glenwood School disappears. RAMONA rises, begins to drop crumbs out of her pocket in imitation of Gretel in the story, as she walks home.)*

SCENE FIVE

(Klickitat Street, and then in the Quimby living room.)

BEEZUS. Ramona! What are you doing? You're making a mess.

RAMONA. My father is a poor woodcutter. In Germany.

BEEZUS. Your father works in a frozen food warehouse. Two miles away. On Grand Avenue near the shopping mall.

RAMONA. I have to leave this trail of crumbs so he can find me at the house of the wicked witch.

BEEZUS. Witch?

RAMONA. Mrs. Griggs. She hates me, Beezus.

BEEZUS. Griggs hates everyone. She's a sourpuss, but she's really not that bad. Just try to go along with her. What are those crumbs?

RAMONA. Peanut butter sandwich cookies.

BEEZUS. Peanut butter?

RAMONA. Hmmm...mmmm.

BEEZUS. Peanut butter doesn't crumb. It's gooey, and you can never get it out of...RAMONA! Don't! *(BEEZUS rushes toward RAMONA to stop her from flicking more crumbs onto the rug, when she skids to a stop. She smells something.)* What's that smell? It smells like burning rubber...Ooooh! My lasagna! The dinner I was making for Aunt Bea...

(BEEZUS rushes off to the kitchen, and MRS. QUIMBY enters, sees her go.)

MRS. QUIMBY. What's wrong?

BEEZUS *(offstage)*. Oh, no!

MRS. QUIMBY. And what's that *smell*? *(She rushes off after BEEZUS.)*

BEEZUS *(offstage)*. Mom! Look what Ramona did!

MRS. QUIMBY *(offstage)*. Oh, Beezus, I'm sorry...

RAMONA *(calling after them)*. Is that wicked witch done yet? *(She skips outside, rushes off down Klickitat Street. She's gone.)*

(BEEZUS and MRS. QUIMBY emerge from the kitchen. MRS. QUIMBY holds the charred corpse of Chevrolet. The body is covered with lasagna.)

MRS. QUIMBY *(furious)*. Ramona! Raaamona!! *(BEEZUS rushes out to the middle of Klickitat Street, looks in every direction.)*

BEEZUS. RAMONA! Ramona, you dork! Where are you?! Come out here! Not only has she ruined my lasagne by dunking Chevrolet in it, but she's gone. Probably lost. Just when I'm baby-sitting for her. RAMONA! RAMONA! RAMONA!? RAMONA? *(No answer.)* I got it. I never should have told her that the world is round like an orange and if you start walking in one direction you'll end up back where you started. She's trying to do it. Ramona's walking around the world. I never told her how big it was. She probably thinks she'll be back by dinner time. She could be across the railroad tracks by now. What'll Mom and Dad say? "Beezus, you pre-teen monster! You lost your precious little sister!" Poor Ramona, trudging miles through scary streets...

(RAMONA appears, walking quietly up behind BEEZUS.)

BEEZUS. ...crossing the big boulevards alone, honked at by trucks and cars, and then up into the mountains, barked at by strange dogs, stalked by grizzly bears, frightened, alone, crying...*(RAMONA taps BEEZUS on the shoulder. BEEZUS jumps with fright, sees RAMONA and is furious.)* Ramona! How could you! How could you ruin my lasagna?

RAMONA. I was playing Gretel, and I burned the witch.

BEEZUS. You got mad 'cause I was making dinner all by myself. Especially with Aunt Bea coming.

RAMONA. So. You wouldn't let me help you.

BEEZUS. You'd make a huge mess.

RAMONA. Would not. I am not a baby.

BEEZUS. It's real grown-up to drown Chevrolet in cheese and tomato sauce.

RAMONA. Stop teasing me! Or I'll tell everyone you have a Cover Girl lipstick in your dresser.

BEEZUS. OOOOH! You are a spying, evil munchkin.

RAMONA. If I am an evil munchkin, you are a Zits Monster. *(That one hurts.)*

BEEZUS. Just go away, you little pest.

(MR. QUIMBY enters, taking off his heavy freezer work clothes. MRS. QUIMBY enters from another room.)

MR. QUIMBY. Not again. Girls, please! I just got home, and I've had a long day.

BEEZUS. But, Daddy, Ramona's being really impossible.

RAMONA. Daddy, it's not fair!

MRS. QUIMBY. Quiet, both of you. *(Silence for a second.)*

RAMONA. Beezus gets to stay up late, and not wear hand-me-downs, and cook, and talk to the audience, and...

MR. QUIMBY. Ramona, you have to...

BEEZUS. Mom! Am I supposed to feel guilty because I'm older?

RAMONA. Beezus'll be President of the United States and a movie star, and I'll still be in Glenwood School and have to be in Mrs. Griggs' class forever.

BEEZUS. My own sister drives me batty. She gets away with everything.

RAMONA. Beezus never shares anything!

(BEA enters. She is carrying a large paper bag with the word WHOPPERBURGER clearly visible on its side. No one notices her. She watches with a smile.)

BEEZUS. You never share anything with me.

RAMONA. You never *want* any of my stuff.

BEEZUS. Who wants chewed up crayons?

RAMONA. Who wants copies of *Teen Beat,* and empty tubes of Clearasil.

BEA. Ladies!

RAMONA and BEEZUS. Aunt Bea!

BEA. Arguing always makes me hungry. How about you? Your mom told me that Chevrolet went scuba-diving in the lasagna, so I thought that stopping by Whopperburger wasn't such a bad idea.

BEEZUS. Aunt Bea, I wish you could have had the dinner I was cooking. It was gonna be soooo good.

BEA. I bet it was. Next time, we'll all have lasagna à la Beezus.

RAMONA (*peering into Whopperburger bag, but still teary and upset*). I love Whopperburgers.

BEA. Ramona, I don't want you to think that if you drop a doll into Beezus' cooking, I'll always bring you a double cheese to go.

RAMONA. But...

BEA. Ramona!

MR. QUIMBY. It's some kind of phase she's going through. I hope.

BEA. I think it's a phase all little sisters go through. (*RA-MONA starts crying. She is sobbing hard, her body shaking.*)

MRS. QUIMBY. What is it now, Ramona? What's wrong?

RAMONA. I can't tell anybody!

MR. QUIMBY. Ramona, you know this family always tries to tell each other what's bothering us...

RAMONA. If I tell, you won't love me anymore.

MR. QUIMBY. Yes, we will.

MRS. QUIMBY. Of course we will.

RAMONA (*blurting it out*). Well...I *hate* Beezus. I know she's my sister, but sometimes I hate hate hate her! (*A moment's silence.*) There. Now everyone knows what a horrible girl I am. *(A silence. Then laughter from GROWN-UPS.)*

MRS. QUIMBY. You're not horrible at all, Ramona.

RAMONA. I'm not?

MRS. QUIMBY. There's no reason why you should love Beezus all the time. I bet there's lots of times when she doesn't love you.

BEEZUS *(full sarcasm)*. Not true. I love Ramona, every golden moment. I love sharing a room with her, I love...

BEA. Beezus! Say it straight, so Ramona won't be confused.

BEEZUS. I don't love Ramona all the time. I do love her sometimes, and sometimes she makes me just plain mad.

BEA *(laughs)*. You know, all sisters have these kinds of battles. Don't they, Dorothy?

MRS. QUIMBY. I'll never forget when you took my beautiful blonde Barbie and dyed her hair with shoe polish. Greasy black. I didn't love you then, not one bit.

BEA. You were always sooo bossy, because you were older. I couldn't wait to grow up and catch up to you...and it seemed like I never would.

MRS. QUIMBY. You were so messy, Bea, you made our room a pigsty. You left your dirty socks on my pillow.

BEA. I never did that.

MRS. QUIMBY. Yes, you did.

BEA. Did not.

MRS. QUIMBY. Did.

BEA. Don't get bossy with me, Dorothy Quimby. *(BEA and MRS. QUIMBY laugh.)* Girls, your mother caught a big frog in the garden and put the slimy thing in *my* clothes drawer.

MRS. QUIMBY. That was only because your Aunt Bea squeezed an entire tube of toothpaste into the batter for my birthday cake. And drew lizards in red crayon in all the books I had from the school library. I had to go to the principal's office!

BEA (*with a grin*). How could I have done such terrible things?

BEEZUS. Aunt Bea, you were every bit as awful as Ramona.

RAMONA. Maybe I should come over and live at your house, Aunt Bea, and we could...

BEA. I don't think so, Ramona. I'm not that messy anymore. But we do have our date for the zoo coming up.

MRS. QUIMBY. Come on, everybody. Our Whopperburger dinner is getting cold...(*ALL except BEEZUS head off toward the dining room. On the way, RAMONA leaps into BEA's arms.*)

BEEZUS (*to audience*). Think about it. Aunt Bea *used to be* every bit as awful as Ramona. And look at her now. There is hope that someday...(*MR. QUIMBY leans back into the room.*)

MR. QUIMBY. Beezus? We love you too, you know.

BEEZUS. Thanks, Dad.

MR. QUIMBY. Come on in and get a burger with the rest of the Quimbys.

BEEZUS (*to MR. QUIMBY*). Don't mind if I do. (*To audience.*) 'Scuse me. I gotta go eat. I'll be back...(*BEEZUS is gone.*)

EN DSR SCENE SIX

(RAMONA's classroom at Glenwood School. Perhaps a dental chart, featuring the friendly tooth family. Three desks/chairs.

HOWIE, RAMONA, and SUSAN are seated. MRS. GRIGGS is in charge. HOWIE looks bored. RAMONA stares vacantly out the window, daydreaming.)

MRS. GRIGGS. Remember, class; Mr. and Mrs....

RAMONA, HOWIE and SUSAN. Canine.

MRS. GRIGGS. Aunt...

RAMONA, HOWIE and SUSAN. Bicuspid.

MRS. GRIGGS. Uncle...

RAMONA, HOWIE and SUSAN. Incisor.

MRS. GRIGGS. ...and Cousin...

RAMONA, HOWIE and SUSAN. Molar.

MRS. GRIGGS. The friendly tooth family. That concludes our unit in dental hygiene. Any questions? *(SUSAN raises her hand.)* Susan?

SUSAN. That was a neat lesson, Mrs. Griggs. I know my teeth much better now.

MRS. GRIGGS. Thank you, Susan. *(HOWIE's hand is up.)* Howie?

HOWIE. What are those big front ones on a vampire called?

MRS. GRIGGS. Vampires aren't really...uh...Why do you ask, Howie?

HOWIE. 'Cause I got some for Halloween. *(Slips vampire fangs into his mouth, turns to audience.)* I'm Count Chocula!

RAMONA. Mrs. Griggs, when do we get to finish our Halloween masks?

SUSAN. You said we'd get to finish them for the Halloween
parade. It's next week.

MRS. GRIGGS. All right, class. Masks out. *(On each desk, a
large mask construction project on a stand appears.
HOWIE has a ferocious vampire. RAMONA has a spooky
owl's head mask. SUSAN's mask is still blank, could be
anything. Mask making music. ALL THREE start working
away with glitter, paste, feathers, scraps of cloth, cardboard, etc.)* Please remember that poor children in Lithua-
nia and Botswana can never make ghosts and goblins to
wear in the Halloween parade because they...have no
paste. If we waste paste, there is...paste waste. *(As MRS.
GRIGGS babbles on, we see SUSAN at a loss, not knowing
what mask to make. She eyes RAMONA's work. RA-
MONA's owl has huge, pointy ears, a giant hooked beak,
and cardboard sunglasses. Before you know it, SUSAN is
making an owl, and it looks a lot like RAMONA's. She's
copying, and copying fast.)*

RAMONA *(under her breath)*. Susan, you're a copycat!
*(SUSAN finishes her work, popping identical cardboard
sunglasses onto her owl head mask. She stands proudly
alongside the finished product. RAMONA is still adding a
few feathers to her own work.)*

MRS. GRIGGS. Look, class! What a scary and unusual owl
Susan has made!

RAMONA *(hesitantly)*. Mrs. Griggs, I...

MRS. GRIGGS. How unusual! How creative! Susan's owl
will fly in the place of honor when all the parents and the
principal visit on Parents Night! *(MRS. GRIGGS hangs
SUSAN's owl from a string, and it flies up high above the
classroom in the place of honor. It twirls about in the
light.)* Why is your owl wearing sunglasses, Susan?

SUSAN. Uh...because it's a very sunny day.

RAMONA. Because a mask and sunglasses are a disguise, and the owl wants to be disguised a lot.

MRS. GRIGGS. Ramona Quimby. How could you know what Susan's owl is doing?

RAMONA. Because I made it up. Look. *(RAMONA waves her own owl mask in front of MRS. GRIGGS.)*

MRS. GRIGGS. Oh, my! Similar ears, similar beak, similar sunglasses. Hmmm. Ramona, you must have copied from Susan. We should all do our own work, even if it's just making masks.

RAMONA. It's not just making masks. It's...it's...art work. I didn't copy. Susan is the copycat, and you made her owl the best in the class.

SUSAN. Ramona is a copycat from me.

MRS. GRIGGS. Ramona, I am disappointed in you. You know better than to lie about...RAMONA!! *(RAMONA has grabbed a yardstick, stands up on her desk, and smashes SUSAN's hanging owl mask into pieces.)* Ramona, stop that at once! Give me that ruler. *(MRS. GRIGGS takes the yardstick away from RAMONA, who defiantly gets down.)* Whoever copied from who, that is no reason to destroy Susan's owl. I want you to apologize. Ramona, do you hear me? *Sit down*

RAMONA. Yes, Mrs. Griggs. *(SUSAN grins in triumph at RAMONA's humiliation.)*

MRS. GRIGGS. I asked you to say you're sorry. *(RAMONA is silent.)* Do you think you can say you're sorry to Susan? *(Long beat.)*

RAMONA. No. I can't.

MRS. GRIGGS. Well, Ramona, then you'll have to go home and stay there—till you can make up your mind to apologize.

RAMONA. Go home now? Right in the middle of school?

MRS. GRIGGS. Yes, Ramona. Right now. *(RAMONA, head down, walks sadly away from Glenwood School.)*

SCENE SEVEN

(Back on Klickitat Street, RAMONA moodily kicks leaves.)

RAMONA. Cross out Ramona. The dumb girl with no future. I'll never learn how to read hard books. Or write cursive. I'll never know how to make paper pilgrim hats 'cause I flunked third grade before Thanksgiving. I'll never learn geography, or social science, whatever that is...

(BEEZUS appears, and looks at RAMONA with sympathy... too much sympathy.)

BEEZUS *(alarmed)*. Ramona, what's bothering you?

RAMONA. I'm a third grade drop-out and I'll have to wash greasy dishes in the back of the Whopperburger all day. And all night.

BEEZUS. Ramona, you aren't making sense.

RAMONA. It makes sense to me, Beezus. I can't go back to school, ever.

BEEZUS. I don't get it.

RAMONA. Nobody does.

SCENE EIGHT

(The Kemp living room. MRS. KEMP is knitting an endless scarf, and watching TV. We hear some of it. Soap opera stuff. RAMONA sits near her, bored and restless.)

MRS. KEMP. Today is a special day, Ramona Quimby.

RAMONA. Why?

MRS. KEMP. My son Hobart is coming home. Howie's uncle, you know. In fact, he's picking Howie up at school on his way in from the airport.

RAMONA. Is he nice, Mrs. Kemp?

MRS. KEMP. He's a wonderful boy. And I'll tell you a secret, Ramona. Hobart made oodles of money in Saudi Arabia...looking for oil or something.

RAMONA. Is he a millionaire?

MRS. KEMP. Well, perhaps he is.

RAMONA. I once saved up four dollars, but I spent it. Does Howie's Uncle Hobart have a big black car and a chauffeur with a hat?

MRS. KEMP. I doubt it, Ramona. That's not like my Hobart.

RAMONA. I bet a millionaire could buy a whole ice cream store, and taste all thirty-seven flavors...Mrs. Kemp?

MRS. KEMP. Yes, Ramona?

RAMONA. If you have a million dollars, can you go to Whopperburger whenever you want to?

MRS. KEMP. Absolutely. As Hobart says, no problemo. *(MRS. KEMP adjusts the TV. We get the audio, with soap opera music under.)*

RAMONA. Is this the soap opera I like, Mrs. Kemp? With the lady in the wheelchair who really loves the doctor, but that man with the beard is so mean to her? *(RAMONA does both voices here—female, then male.)* "Don't hurt me,

Robert! I love you!" "You lying little tramp. You're not really sick. Get up and walk." "I can't. Oh, Robert, Robert, I can't! Ooooh..." *(RAMONA imitates a wheelchair patient struggling to get up, and then falling to the floor. She twitches, and then lies there.)*

MRS. KEMP. Ramona, you can't continue to stay home and watch TV all day. It's not good for your mind.

RAMONA. You do it.

MRS. KEMP. I'm a grown-up, Ramona. And I already went to school.

RAMONA. I want to go to school with Howie, but I can't. They all hate me, and they think I'm a copycat, and it's not fair.

MRS. KEMP. Nonsense, Ramona.

RAMONA. Nobody understands. *(A horn sounds, beeps of arrival.)* The millionaire! I bet he has a tuxedo, and gold shoes!

(In a moment, HOWIE and his bearded UNCLE HOBART enter.)

HOBART. MOM!

MRS. KEMP. Oh, Hobart! Let me see you. *(She gets out of her chair, and they embrace.)*

HOBART. Mom, you look wonderful!

MRS. KEMP. You look thin. What have they been feeding you?

HOBART. Camel tongue and hummingbird eggs.

MRS. KEMP. I knew it! You haven't had a good meal since you left home. I'll make all your favorites and apple pie for dessert.

HOBART. I fell asleep every night dreaming of your apple pie! *(Glances at TV.)* Weren't you watching that same show when I left home ten years ago? *(Turning suddenly to RAMONA.)* And who is this young lady? Howie! You didn't tell me you had a girlfriend. Shame on you.

HOWIE. That's not my...

RAMONA. I am not Howie's girlfriend. I have to stay here with Mrs. Kemp till my mother is back from shopping. It's strictly business.

HOBART *(laughs)*. Miss Not-Howie's-girlfriend, I'm Howie's uncle, Hobart Kemp. Pleased to meet you. *(Exaggerated bow.)* You are...

RAMONA. Ramona. From next door.

HOBART. Ramona? Ramona...*(Sings and dances romantically.)* Ramona, I hear the mission bells above, Ramona, they're ringing out our song of love.

RAMONA *(embarrassed by this teasing coming from an adult)*. Mr. Kemp, stop that. Grown-ups shouldn't...*(HOBART doesn't notice. He's having too much fun, and sails on.)*

HOBART. I dread the dawn, when I awake to find you gone, Ramona, Ramona, my loooooovvveee!!!!! *(RAMONA looks away, confused and upset.)* What's the matter, Ramona?

HOWIE. Cut it out, Uncle Hobart.

HOBART. Don't you like songs about you?

RAMONA. I don't like grown-ups who're mean and tease kids.

MRS. KEMP. Ramona! Manners!

HOBART. Now, Mom, don't get excited. No problem. Ramona has a point. I was teasing, but I intend to reform.

RAMONA. Howie, do you think it's fair that some people have a bazillion dollars, and my dad has to work very hard in the cold at the FrostKing Frozen Foods warehouse?

HOBART. It's not fair, Ramona. It's just how it is.

RAMONA. Well, it shouldn't be that way.

MRS. KEMP. What is the matter with you, Ramona Quimby?

HOBART. Quimby? Are you Ramona Quimby? With a mom who has a sister named Bea?

(Lights up in BEA's apartment. She comes to the window, looks out over the city toward Klickitat Street. Music plays, far away.)

RAMONA. Bea? Hmmmm...No. Nobody named Bea in my family.

HOWIE. Ramona, how could you forget your Aunt Bea? You never stop talking about her apartment, and her yellow convertible.

HOBART. The Bea I used to know was a yellow convertible kind of girl. She was in my class at Glenwood School, many moons ago.

RAMONA. Aunt Bea moved to Los Angeles. Just yesterday.

HOBART *(not believing her for a moment)*. That's too bad. *(BEA's light goes out. She's gone.)*

(MRS. QUIMBY appears in her living room, along with BEEZUS and MR. QUIMBY. They all look serious.)

MR. QUIMBY *(calling)*. Ramonaaa!

RAMONA. Goodbye, Mr. Kemp. So long, Howie. 'Bye, Mrs. Kemp. *(RAMONA heads for her own house, her family.)*

HOBART *(singing softly)*. Ramona, I hear the mission bells above...*(RAMONA glances back at HOBART, sticks her tongue out at him. He stops singing, sticks his tongue out in return.)*

SCENE NINE

(The Quimby living room. RAMONA, BEEZUS, MR. and MRS. QUIMBY.)

MR. QUIMBY. Finish your chores?

RAMONA. Uh...uh.

MRS. QUIMBY. Yes?

RAMONA. If I stay away from school long enough, even Mrs. Griggs will forget who I am, and then I can go back and she'll think I'm someone else.

MRS. QUIMBY. Ramona, Mrs. Griggs will never think you're someone else. I went to school and talked to her today.

RAMONA. You what?

MRS. QUIMBY. She sent you a note. *(Hands it to RA-MONA.)*

RAMONA. She did? *(Opening the envelope. Reading slowly.)* "Dear Ramona Q., We all miss you. Please come back to third grade soon. Signed, Mrs. Griggs." Maybe she does like me, a little. Does she still want me to apologize to Susan?

MRS. QUIMBY. I'm afraid she does.

RAMONA. She's wrong, Mama. Susan copied me, and Mrs. Griggs put Susan's owl up for Parents Day. And Susan lied, and she even wasted paste.

MR. QUIMBY. That still doesn't make it okay for you to smash Susan's owl.

RAMONA. I just got sooo mad.

MRS. QUIMBY. Susan is the one I feel sorry for. You're the one who can think up her own ideas. You have a wonderful imagination.

RAMONA. Maybe I do, but that doesn't help me now.

MR. QUIMBY. Someday it will. Ramona, listen to me. You must go back to school, my little sparkler, and apologize.

RAMONA. Do I have to?

MR. QUIMBY. Yes, Ramona. You do.

RAMONA. It isn't fair, Daddy.

MR. QUIMBY. Ramona, sometimes life isn't fair.

RAMONA. It isn't fair that life isn't fair.

MR. QUIMBY. Ramona, it's bedtime. Tomorrow morning you go to school.

MRS. QUIMBY. Tomorrow night is the Halloween parade.

MR. QUIMBY. And after the parade, we all go to the Whopperburger!

RAMONA. Really?!

MR. QUIMBY. We'll get orange hamburgers and black French fries.

RAMONA. Cross your heart and hope to die about the Whopperburger?

MR. QUIMBY. You got it.

RAMONA. Tomorrow's a school day, so I've got to get to bed. Good night, everybody. *(She turns and walks off to bed, with a little spring in her step. Silence.)*

BEEZUS *(turns to her PARENTS)*. Mrs. Griggs was always big on apologies.

SCENE TEN

(HOWIE in voice over as we cross fade to Glenwood School.

MRS. GRIGGS, SUSAN, RAMONA, and HOWIE, who is at the end of his Show and Tell. He is wearing a child's floor-length Arab burnoose.)

HOWIE *(embarrassed)*. …and my Uncle Hobart says that all the boys in Saudi Arabia wear long dresses. He brought this one back for me. I hate wearing it, but my grandma thought it would be good for Show and Tell. That's all. *(SUSAN giggles. HOWIE returns to his seat, taking off the embarrassing garment as he goes. A moment's silence.)*

MRS. GRIGGS. Thank you for sharing, Howie. I believe that Ramona has something to say to us.

RAMONA. I don't have anything for Show and Tell today, Mrs. Griggs.

MRS. GRIGGS. But you do have something to say to Susan.

RAMONA. Now? In front of the whole class…

MRS. GRIGGS. We're waiting. *(SUSAN beams with satisfaction. RAMONA is in agony, but finally, she grits her teeth, stands, walks closer to SUSAN's desk.)*

RAMONA. Susan, I'm sorry I smashed your owl.

SUSAN. It was horrible, but I forgive you.

MRS. GRIGGS. Thank you, Ramona Q. I know we're all glad you're back in school. Excuse me, class. *(MRS. GRIGGS is gone for a moment, perhaps behind the American flag in the schoolroom. Once she is out of the way…)*

RAMONA *(very sweetly)*. Psssst! Susan!

SUSAN *(leans toward RAMONA)*. Yes?

RAMONA. You're still a copycat, and a rotten, stinky dinosaur egg! *(MRS. GRIGGS emerges from hiding. She wears a full and frightening Gypsy costume.)*

MRS. GRIGGS. GET YOUR COSTUMES!!! HALLOWEEN PARADE!

SCENE ELEVEN

(Music, energetic, loud, and fizzy goblin music. Dance sequence in wonderful Halloween costumes, with the entire CAST, including SCOUTS et al. If this "parade" has a story line [i.e., monsters trying to scare an innocent victim, or two groups of different monsters scaring each other]— all the better. During the sequence, RAMONA attempts to pull SUSAN's hair, pulls HOWIE's instead. All sorts of strange creatures appear. HOWIE wears his vampire mask plus cape, SUSAN wears a fairy princess outfit, and RA-MONA is dressed as a witch.

The last spook seems to have gone, music fades, a small WITCH leaps out at the audience and cackles.)

RAMONA AS WITCH. Haa! Haa! Haa! *(Music crash, and out. Dance sequence over. Glenwood School is gone.)*

SCENE TWELVE

(The FrostKing Frozen Foods warehouse. Snow falls. A sign, if needed, with icy lettering: FROSTKING FROZEN FOODS.

MR. QUIMBY appears, carrying a pile of frozen turkeys, hung with icicles. He wears his hat with earflaps, and a heavy coat. MR. FROST appears in this icy world; he is a large man with a full white beard, wearing a huge fur coat and sunglasses.)

MR. FROST. Quimby!

MR. QUIMBY. Oh, hello there, Mr. Frost.

MR. FROST. Quimby, orders are down. You're a good man, Quimby, but I'm closing this entire freezehouse. YOU'RE FIRED! *(The snow stops falling. Lights grow warmer. Icicles melt.)*

MR. QUIMBY. But, Mr. Frost, my family can't...

MR. FROST. Good luck, Quimby. The way things are these days, you'll need it.

SCENE THIRTEEN

(MR. FROST and his warehouse are gone, and MR. QUIMBY, dropping his heavy outer clothes, heads for the Quimby living room, where MRS. QUIMBY, BEEZUS, and RAMONA are gathered. The mood is solemn.)

MR. QUIMBY. No gold watch, no two weeks' notice. Just canned.

RAMONA. Daddy, he can't do that to you.

MR. QUIMBY. Yes he can, my little sparkler. And he did. I'm out of a job, Dorothy. And we've got a stack of bills this high.

MRS. QUIMBY. You'll find something else soon. I know you will. And the girls'll help me stretch the savings we've got.

BEEZUS. I guess this means no Whopperburger tonight.

RAMONA. But I wanted to...

MRS. QUIMBY. Sorry, Ramona. This family won't be going to the Whopperburger for a while. We can eat more economically at home.

RAMONA. What's economically?

MR. QUIMBY. Leftovers.

BEEZUS. We learned in my social science class that a recession exists in this part of the country.

MR. QUIMBY. You can tell your class it came right into your living room, and sat down on the couch.

RAMONA. Does this mean you're not gonna go to the North Pole and be Santa's helper ever again?

MR. QUIMBY. I never really liked being Santa's helper anyway. It was cold in there.

RAMONA. We're all going to be homeless and live in a refrigerator box.

MRS. QUIMBY. What?

RAMONA. I saw it on TV.

MRS. QUIMBY. Ramona, don't be silly.

RAMONA. I'm not being silly. I'm being scared.

BEEZUS. We have to keep making house payments, you know. If Daddy isn't working...

MRS. QUIMBY. I don't want you girls to worry. Daddy and I will work this out.

(The phone rings. In the distance, BEA's apartment window lights up. She's on the phone.)

RAMONA. I'll get it! Hello?

BEA *(strange voice).* Ramona! This is the queen of the Planet Mongo!

RAMONA. It is not. It's my Aunt Bea.

BEA *(own voice).* Caught me again. Ramona, I have some good news and some bad news. The good news is...I'll be at your house later in the week for dinner, with a fabulous surprise.

RAMONA. Surprise?!?! What?!?

BEA. You'll see. The bad news is...something's come up and I can't take you to the zoo tomorrow.

RAMONA. But you promised.

BEA. I'm sorry, Ramona. I just can't. I'll see you soon, though. 'Bye.

RAMONA (sadly). 'Bye...(She hangs up, and BEA and her apartment are gone.) Aunt Bea isn't taking me to the zoo.

MR. QUIMBY. Ramona, it must be something pretty important or Aunt Bea wouldn't break a date with you.

RAMONA. She probably thinks I'm a pest, and a little whiny third grader.

MRS. QUIMBY. She thinks you're her marvelous little Ramona, who is the brightest and most unboring niece she could ever have.

RAMONA. She does?

MRS. QUIMBY. Yes, she does. Time for you to wash your hands and help Beezus set the table.

RAMONA (wistful). Beezus wouldn't have to set the table if we went to the Whopperburger...

MRS. QUIMBY. Things will get better for us sometime. (MRS. QUIMBY kisses RAMONA.) I promise.

SCENE FOURTEEN

(Ramona's bedroom and, downstage of it, Klickitat Street. A dim light is on in Ramona's room, and a wakeful RA-MONA is looking out onto the nighttime street.)

SCENE FIFTEEN

(Lights up on the Quimby living room. MRS. QUIMBY and BEEZUS are putting the finishing touches on a pretty buffet table off to one side that is set with food for dinner. Candles in holders.)

BEEZUS. It's just not right to have Aunt Bea over and give her Hamburger Helper and vegetable soup made from whatever was in the refrigerator that had wilted. When we go there she gives us quiche and ginger ale and...

MRS. QUIMBY. Beezus, would you set out that silverware?

BEEZUS. ...and roast beef sandwiches on French bread with butter and...

MRS. QUIMBY. Beezus, please don't complain. Remember, Bea is a single woman with a full-time teaching job and enough money to buy you kids presents when you visit once a month. She doesn't buy your clothes, and food, and take care of your *entire life*.

(MR. QUIMBY and RAMONA enter. RAMONA has her party best on. The doorbell rings, and RAMONA rushes to greet BEA, who's a little dressier than usual, with a flower in her hair. RAMONA checks her over for the big surprise. She's not carrying any packages.)

RAMONA. She's here! Aunt Bea! Where's my surprise?

BEA. The surprise is for everyone, and it's parking the car down the street. *(Looking offstage.)* It's coming closer... closer...Here it is!

(HOBART enters with a flourish. He's also a little dressier than usual, but not much. Maybe a flower in the lapel of the jacket he wears.)

HOBART. Hi!

BEA. Uncle Hobart, all the way from next door. We've renewed an old high school friendship over the past few days. Hobart, meet the best older sister a girl could have.

HOBART *(to MRS. QUIMBY)*. Charmed and delighted.

MR. QUIMBY. I'm Bob Quimby.

HOBART. My pleasure. And you must be Beezus. *(Kisses her hand.)*

BEEZUS. Gosh!

HOBART. I've already met Ramona. She doesn't care for my singing, so I'm on my best behavior.

RAMONA. Haven't you gone back to Saudi Arabia on a camel yet, Mr. Kemp?

HOBART. Miss Ramona Quimby, are you trying to get rid of me?

RAMONA. You're the "something" that made me miss my trip to the zoo.

MRS. QUIMBY. Ramona, be polite.

RAMONA. I'm trying.

MRS. QUIMBY. Try harder.

HOBART. As a matter of fact, I'm not going back to Saudi at all. I'm heading up to Alaska.

BEA. Mush, you huskies! North Pole ahead! Santa's workshop!

HOBART. It'll be a great opportunity. The geologists tell me there are new oil fields up there that look promising. *(MRS. QUIMBY and BEEZUS light candles on the buffet table. It's as romantic as they could make it on a limited budget.)*

MRS. QUIMBY. Ladies and gentlemen, help yourselves.

BEA. Dorothy, it looks beautiful. *(RAMONA rushes over to the table first, looks at the various dishes, turns to the group.)*

RAMONA. And, for dessert, Fig Newtons full of chopped up worms.

BEEZUS. That's disgusting.

MRS. QUIMBY. Ramona, that's quite enough. Some days, I don't know what to do with you.

RAMONA *(smiling—knowing this won't happen)*. Lock me in the closet for a million years. Give me nothing but stale bread and water.

MR. QUIMBY *(strongly)*. Ramona! If you can't take a plate of food, and then join in the conversation like a grown-up, you'll go to your room and stay there. *(As ALL help themselves, and sit around the living room, RAMONA goes quietly off into a downstage corner. BEA approaches, sits down next to her. RAMONA is crestfallen. She knows she has gone too far.)*

RAMONA. I don't like your surprise one bit.

BEA. Ramona, Hobart is very sweet once you get to know him.

RAMONA. I don't want to get to know him. He teases kids.

BEA. Really? I think he's reformed. You'll see. You still mad at me about the zoo?

RAMONA. No.

BEA. I think you might be, just a little.

RAMONA. Well, I am. Lots. I even had a bad dream about it. I was at the zoo all alone, in just my underwear. Everyone was laughing at me, even the animals.

BEA. I've had a dream like that. I was in just my underwear and sneakers in a crowded shopping mall. I don't know how I got there, right in front of a pizza stand. Everyone was staring and laughing. I was sooo embarrassed.

RAMONA *(seriously)*. Did you ever dream your bed was flying?

BEA. All the time. Ramona, that's one of my favorites. We might do a lot of the same dreaming. Maybe our beds will meet some night in the sky, high above Klickitat Street. *(BEEZUS pulls MRS. QUIMBY downstage.)*

MRS. QUIMBY. All right, Beezus!

BEEZUS. Aunt Bea, Mom has something to tell you!

MRS. QUIMBY. Bea, Hobart...I have an announcement to make. One that's long overdue. As of tomorrow, there'll be one less housewife in America. I'm going out to look for a job.

BEA. Dorothy, that's great news. Take the chain off the stove!

BEEZUS. Mom! You're liberated!

MRS. QUIMBY. Thank you, Beezus.

RAMONA. That's easy for Beezus to say, but who'll take care of me when I come home from school? Or if I get sick?

MR. QUIMBY. We've arranged it with Mrs. Kemp.

RAMONA. Mrs. Kemp—oh, yuk!

MRS. QUIMBY. Ramona!

HOBART. No problem.

MRS. QUIMBY. She's perfectly nice, Ramona. You don't hate her. You need to get used to staying with her after school.

RAMONA. Who'll bake cookies if you're gone all day?

MRS. QUIMBY. You can, Ramona. You're old enough.

RAMONA *(solemnly)*. I'll burn myself. I'll get blisters all over my hands.

MRS. QUIMBY. Not if you're careful. *(RAMONA gets up from the table, terribly unhappy.)*

RAMONA. Why don't you just *give* me to Mrs. Kemp? I'll be her daughter, and watch soap operas all day.

MR. QUIMBY. Ramona, this family is trying to stay together under this roof, and be warm and dry. You have to help, even if you don't like it. Being grownup means doing things you *need* to do, that maybe you don't want to do— for a while anyway. (*RAMONA turns her back on the family, goes over to the window.*)

RAMONA (*to herself*). I don't want to grow up—not yet. I'm not old enough.

SCENE SIXTEEN

BEEZUS. It's winter on Klickitat Street. We've gotta wear sweaters in the house these days to keep the heat low, 'cause of the fuel bill. Not only do we never get to go to Whopperburger anymore, we have to eat disgusting things like tongue because it's cheap and nutritious. Yuk! I hate tongue. I can tell Mom and Dad are worried 'cause they whisper all the time and have long, serious discussions with the door closed. I know they think we're too young to understand but it really feels awful when they shut us out like that. And it feels even worse knowing my family is in trouble and there's nothing I can do to help.

(*RAMONA looks out onto Klickitat Street. It's a winter evening, street light and shadows. Some light snow falls. The OLD MAN with the straw hat, out for a stroll, spots RAMONA at the window. He salutes, and he's gone. As he exits, a troop of CUB SCOUTS with blue flashlights enters past him, almost knocking him over. From the opposite*

*side of the stage, the BROWNIES enter, their flashlight
beams bright pink. Little dance of the flashlights as RA-
MONA watches. They all click out. Darkness.*

*Klickitat Street transforms itself from night to day, and
loses all its spookiness. Some snow lies on the ground.
BEEZUS, now in jacket and hat, steps toward the audience.)*

BEEZUS. Guess what? Today my *mom* got a job.

SCENE SEVENTEEN

*(In another area, a DOCTOR zooms onstage in a white
chair on wheels attached to a little table holding a white
telephone with a red cross on it. He is fully out-fitted including head reflector. MRS. QUIMBY joins him. He gets
up out of the rolling chair.)*

DOCTOR. YOU'RE HIRED! *(The DOCTOR exits. The
phone rings. MRS. QUIMBY picks it up.)*
MRS. QUIMBY. Dr. Mitchell's office. *(Phone rings again.)*
Please hold. *(Hits button, sits in chair.)* Dr. Mitchell's of-
fice. Next Thursday? I'll...*(Phone rings.)* Please hold.
(Phone rings.) Dr. Mitchell's office...Me? Dorothy
Quimby. I'm the new receptionist. *(Rings.)* Please hold.
(Blackout on DOCTOR's office.)

SCENE EIGHTEEN

(Klickitat Street.)

BEEZUS. Mom's at work. She's working hard, but money is still tight at our house. I've got homework to do over at Pamela's, so Ramona's home alone with Dad.

(RAMONA appears, sitting on the floor in the Quimby living room. She wears a sweater. Alongside her is MR. QUIMBY, who stares dully into the TV. There is another large monitor on high, so we can see the TV action at times. MR. QUIMBY wears a sweater as well. He is smoking a cigarette.)

BEEZUS. Dad still looks for work, but he hasn't had much luck. He mostly sits home and watches TV. Just like Mrs. Kemp, except...I hate to tell this part, but *(Looking over at MR. QUIMBY smoking a cigarette.)* it's pretty obvious. Dad started smoking again. He's up to a pack a day. Marlboros. I told him to stop. I told Ramona to tell him to stop. It's stupid, that's all. I know he's my dad, but he's acting stupid. He'll just die, and then we'll all cry, and be sad for months and years and forever. Dad should think of us. *(BEEZUS puts up a handmade NO SMOKING sign. She exits.)*

SCENE NINETEEN

(The Quimby living room. Afternoon. MR. QUIMBY and RAMONA watch soap operas on TV, we can hear snatches of the soapy dialogue. MR. QUIMBY smokes. TV, with soap music, fades under...)

RAMONA. Dad, are we gonna go to a shelter?

MR. QUIMBY. No, honey. We're staying right here.

RAMONA. I heard Mom say it's hard to get money for the house payments.

MR. QUIMBY. Ramona, *please.* Don't worry.

RAMONA. Dad, if you could have any job in the whole world, what would you pick?

MR. QUIMBY. I'd like to be a teacher, Ramona. Maybe right at your school.

RAMONA. You'd be the best teacher ever. Way better than Mrs. Griggs.

MR. QUIMBY. Maybe, Ramona. But I'd need to go to college first, and we can't afford for me not to work—for a while, anyway.

RAMONA. I could baby-sit.

MR. QUIMBY. Ramona, you still need a baby-sitter yourself.

RAMONA. Dad, if we don't have much money, how come you can pay for cigarettes?

MR. QUIMBY. My smoking is none of your business.

RAMONA. Beezus says it's my business.

MR. QUIMBY. Beezus needs a talking to. *(RAMONA grabs the pack of Marlboros from his shirt pocket, holds them behind her back. He chases after, tries to get them.)* Ramona, give those back to me. Ramona! *(She flings them off the stage.)*

RAMONA. There.

MR. QUIMBY. That is a waste of money, Ramona—you know you shouldn't destroy other people's property. You don't understand.

RAMONA. Yes, I do. Your lungs'll turn black and you'll die, and you'll be dead before I grow up, and you won't see me graduate from junior high or anything. If you promise to *try* to stop, I won't grab your cigarettes or throw them away.

MR. QUIMBY. I'll tell you what, Ramona. I'll try. For one week, I won't smoke, no matter what. One week, and then we'll see.

(BEEZUS appears, with another hand-lettered NO SMOK-ING sign.)

BEEZUS. Good work, Ramona! It's a start. *(She hangs the sign up on a nearby part of the set, and she's gone. MR. QUIMBY turns the TV up. A commercial comes on. We see it on the large screen above. COMMERCIAL: A BOY Ramona's age holds a burger in his hand, and dances in front of a giant glossy WHOPPERBURGER sign.)*

BOY IN COMMERCIAL *(sings and dances).*
    Forget your pots, forget your pans
    It's not too late to change your plans
    Spend a little, eat a *lot (Big spin and split move.)*
    Big fat burgers, nice and hot
    At your nearest Whopperburger! *(Leap up.)*
    (Taking a big bite.) Wow! Tastes fabulous!

RAMONA *(jealous).* That boy's got a Whopperburger, *with* cheese.

MR. QUIMBY. Never mind the burger. Do you know how much *money* that kid makes for singing that stupid song and saying "Wow, tastes fabulous"?

RAMONA. Ten dollars?

MR. QUIMBY. Maybe a million dollars. I see him singing
that jingle every time I turn on the TV.

RAMONA. He looks like he's in third grade. How can he get
a million dollars?

MR. QUIMBY. They make a movie of him singing that jingle, and then every time it shows on TV, he gets paid. It all
adds up.

RAMONA. If we had a million dollars, could we turn up the
thermostat?

MR. QUIMBY. Ramona. If we had a million dollars we could
heat the garage. It's a fantasy. It's not gonna happen. The
only offer I've got so far is from the Foodtown Market, but
I'm not working in a check-out line with a lot of teen-
agers.

RAMONA. How did he get the job?

MR. QUIMBY. Who?

RAMONA. The Whopperburger boy.

MR. QUIMBY. By dancing, singing, smiling all the time and
being extremely cute, I guess.

RAMONA. But who gave him the job?

MR. QUIMBY. Maybe his teacher or a neighbor told a talent
scout about him. You want some popcorn?

RAMONA. Okay.

MR. QUIMBY. Be back in a minute. *(He gets up and leaves
the room. RAMONA sits in front of the dead TV. She's
thoughtful.)*

RAMONA *(talking to herself).* Dad wouldn't need a stupid
old job, and Mom could be home and bake cookies. We
could even go to Disneyland. *(RAMONA stands, then
sings, and dances. She's smiling powerfully, and holding
her hat in place of the Whopperburger with cheese. She's*

doing her best to become an obnoxious TV child, and al-
most succeeding...)

    Forget your pots, forget your pans

    It's not too late to change your plans

    Spend a little, eat a *lot...*

(RAMONA goes for the leap and split move, but it's a lot
harder than she anticipated, and she comes down in a
heap, everything crooked. Dispirited, and sarcastic...)

    Wow. Tastes fabulous.

(RAMONA hits the remote, and the TV is back. She scans
for commercials. She's got one for NON-SKID PANTY-
HOSE. COMMERCIAL: Distant calliope music. MOTHER,
and CHILD Ramona's age at the zoo, looking at the ele-
phant.)

RAMONA. This one's got a girl in it! *(The CHILD, a per-*
fectly cute, smiling little blonde girl, glances down at her
MOTHER's ankles, then up at the elephant's wrinkled gray
leg skin.)

CHILD. Mommy! Your pantyhose are all wrinkled! Your legs
look like the elephant's! *(Laughs.)*

MOTHER *(looking down at her bagging pantyhose).* You're
right, darling. I should have worn Non-Skid, the never-slip
pantyhose.

CHILD. With Non-Skid, you'd never look like an elephant
again! *(Cue to the ELEPHANT, who nods his great head*
wisely in agreement. Calliope music up and out. RAMONA
is thinking seriously.)

RAMONA *(to herself).* I could do that. I know I could. *(As*
she slips into fantasy, the stage darkens, and the TV moni-
tor flips on of its own accord.)

SCENE TWENTY

*(On TV: RAMONA'S FANTASY COMMERCIAL: It's the
same commercial we just saw, but instead of the original
MOTHER-DAUGHTER, it's RAMONA and MRS.
QUIMBY. Same music, same zoo, but now the ELEPHANT
is a huge elephant puppet/costume.)*

DIRECTOR. C'mon, people! Lights! Roll it!

CAMERA OPERATOR. Speed!

DIRECTOR. Slate! And...action!

RAMONA. Mommy! Your pantyhose! Your legs look just
like the elephant's! All wrinkly and droopy.

MRS. QUIMBY. Ramona, you're extra smart *and* cute. I
should have worn Non-Skid pantyhose.

RAMONA. Then you'd never look like an elephant again!
(Close-up of the ELEPHANT.)

ELEPHANT. That's right, Ramona! *(The ELEPHANT trum-
pets his further agreement. The commercial ends, but the
camera pulls back until the scene reveals the CAMERA
CREW, the DIRECTOR, a Hollywood type with sunglasses,
and the SPONSOR: the President of Non-skid Pantyhose, a
man with a cigar.)*

DIRECTOR. Aaaannnnddd...CUT! And Print! LUNCH! Ramona, darling! You're not a bratty third grader at all!

RAMONA. I'm not?

DIRECTOR. No. You're a great actress!

SPONSOR. Women all over the world are buying Non-Skid
Pantyhose, thanks to you. Here's ONE MILLION DOL-
LARS! *(Close-up of one million dollars being handed to
RAMONA as she stuffs the bills into her pockets, socks,
everywhere—and the TV flips off.)*

(Lights up. RAMONA is asleep in MR. QUIMBY's armchair, a smile on her face. MRS. QUIMBY enters, sees her.)

MRS. QUIMBY. Ramona! *(As she wakes.)* Ramona, you fell asleep. Do you feel okay?

RAMONA. I'm fine, Mommy. *(Big fake smile.)*

MRS. QUIMBY. Why are you calling me mommy? You always call me mom. And why are you smiling like that?

RAMONA. Just practicing. *(The Quimby house is gone.)*

SCENE TWENTY-ONE

(Glenwood School. It's a quiet moment in class. SUSAN, HOWIE, RAMONA. MRS. GRIGGS is watching as the class does seatwork. Her pantyhose are baggy around the ankles. RAMONA comes up to her, a huge insincere smile on her face, skipping like a model child in front of a picket fence. MRS. GRIGGS is naturally suspicious.)

SUSAN. Is that the correct answer, Mrs. Griggs?

MRS. GRIGGS. It certainly is, Susan. Thank you for demonstrating. Now, let's all work on our fractions. Yes, Ramona?

RAMONA. Hi, Mrs. Griggs! You have wrinkled legs, like an elephant! *(Forced laughter, imitating the commercial. SUSAN and HOWIE can't help laughing. MRS. GRIGGS looks down at the pantyhose bagging around her ankles, then stares at this strange new RAMONA.)* With Non-Skid Pantyhose, you'd never look like an elephant again! *(Big smile.)*

MRS. GRIGGS. Ramona, take your seat immediately.

RAMONA. Are you gonna tell a talent scout about me?

MRS. GRIGGS. Ramona, I said take your seat. *(RAMONA heads dejectedly back to her seat, then turns again to MRS. GRIGGS.)*

RAMONA. Wasn't I cute enough?

MRS. GRIGGS. I'm going to have a talk with your parents about this behavior. *(A bell rings. School's out.)* Don't run, children! *(The CHILDREN run like mad, MRS. GRIGGS tugs up her pantyhose, and Glenwood school fades.)*

change into wedding clothes

SCENE TWENTY-TWO

(The Kemp living room. MRS. KEMP is knitting and watching the soaps as usual. RAMONA rushes in.)

RAMONA *(huge smile)*. Mrs. Kemp, how *are* you?

MRS. KEMP. I'm fine, Ramona.

RAMONA *(still smiling powerfully)*. And how is your wonderful son, Howie's Uncle Hobart from Saudi Arabia, who is going to Alaska?

MRS. KEMP. Ramona, why is your face twisted up like that?

RAMONA. That's my smile. Your legs are all wrinkled, just like an elephant's! *(Forced laugh.)*

MRS. KEMP. Ramona, that's extremely rude.

SCENE TWENTY-THREE

(RAMONA spots BEA and HOBART through the Kemp's window, walking down Klickitat Street. HOBART's arm is around BEA's waist. It's spring now. First daffodils.

MRS. KEMP shakes her head in disbelief, as RAMONA rushes off to BEA and HOBART. As she nears them they suddenly embrace! HOBART picks BEA up, and spins her around in circles. They are both laughing joyfully.)

RAMONA. Aunt Bea! Aunt Bea, do you know any talent...

HOBART *(sings loudly)*. Ramona! Hear the mission bells above...

RAMONA. Stop! You know I don't like that song!

BEA. Hobart, stop your silly teasing.

HOBART. Okay. Instead of singing, I'll ask a question. Ramona, how would you like to have me for an uncle?

RAMONA. You're already Howie's uncle.

HOBART. I would like to have a couple of ready-made nieces—you and Beezus.

RAMONA. How could you be our uncle?

HOBART. No problem. All I have to do is marry your Aunt Beatrice. *(BEA laughs, along with HOBART.)*

RAMONA. You mean...

BEA. We're getting married in two weeks, before we leave for Alaska.

RAMONA. You're leaving! Oh, Aunt Bea, how could you? What about the zoo? And Christmas at our house? And where'll you go for Thanksgiving?

BEA. I don't know, Ramona. I haven't thought about all that yet.

RAMONA. What will you *do* in Alaska?

HOBART. She'll build us an igloo. Fish through the ice. Ride a moose.

BEA. Don't listen to him. I'm planning to teach. They *have* schools up there, you know.

(BEEZUS appears. She's heard the news, and is in romantic bliss.)

BEEZUS. Aunt Bea, I just know your wedding'll be soooo beautiful. All the flowers, and music. "Here comes the..."

BEA. Sorry, Beezus. No wedding.

BEEZUS. No wedding?

BEA. Just a Justice of the Peace at City Hall.

BEEZUS. But *why?*

HOBART. A fancy wedding's just not that important.

BEA *(regretfully)*. Hobart's right. Besides, two weeks just isn't enough time to put together a wedding...*(With longing.)*...the food, the guests, the flowers, the dresses...Girls, your mother had a beautiful wedding.

HOBART. But your mother never left Klickitat Street. I have to be in Alaska in two weeks, and we have cars to sell, packing to do, jobs to quit, and people to say goodbye to. No wedding, girls. A lot of love, but no wedding. *(HOBART and BEA exit. RAMONA is dejected.)*

RAMONA. Aunt Bea is leaving me...

BEEZUS. She's leaving *us*. But she'll visit.

RAMONA. No she won't. Uncle Hobart doesn't like me.

BEEZUS. He just likes to tease. Ramona, you wouldn't want Aunt Bea to stay and be unhappy, would you?

RAMONA. Yes, I would!

BEEZUS. That is really super selfish, Ramona.

RAMONA. I don't care. And everyone makes fun of my commercials, so I'll never make the million dollars...

BEEZUS. A million dollars?

RAMONA. To be on TV. I was practicing.

BEEZUS. Ramona, that's dumb. Nobody goes on TV from Klickitat Street. They make TV in Los Angeles. Far away.

RAMONA. I was trying. I just got it all wrong. Aunt Bea is leaving, and Mom works all the time...and...You're my big sister, Beezus. I need a hug.

BEEZUS. No. I'm still mad at you for being so selfish about Aunt Bea. *(BEEZUS self-righteously turns away from RA-MONA. RAMONA, in response, deliberately steps toward the audience.)*

RAMONA *(to audience)*. Beezus has a red lipstick and bikini panties in her dresser.

BEEZUS. Oooooh! Ramona, that's not fair.

RAMONA. Life isn't fair. I'm gonna tell Dad you wouldn't hug me. *(Lights up on the Quimby living room as RA-MONA heads toward it.)*

SCENE TWENTY-FOUR

(MR. QUIMBY is revealed, furtively smoking a cigarette. RAMONA spots him. She is shocked.)

RAMONA. You promised! You promised you wouldn't! *(MR. QUIMBY stubs out the cigarette, and sits down in his chair. He's been caught, and he feels guilty, and weak.)*

MR. QUIMBY. Ramona, I tried. Believe me, I tried.

RAMONA. Daddy, you were *cheating*.

MR. QUIMBY. Ramona, it's hard to break a bad habit.

RAMONA. You promised a week!

MR. QUIMBY. I ran across one cigarette, an old stale one in my coat pocket, and thought it might help the way I was feeling if I smoked it. It didn't—and I broke my promise. I'm sorry. I want you to feel your dad's the best—but that's just not true all the time.

RAMONA. Daddy, there's a lot of things I try that I can't do...till I get a little stronger. I didn't know grown-ups had that trouble too.

MR. QUIMBY. This grown-up does. *(RAMONA hugs her FA-THER.)*

RAMONA. I love you, Daddy. Nobody can do things right every time. And I love you for trying.

MR. QUIMBY. Same to you, my little sparkler.

(MRS. QUIMBY and BEEZUS enter together, stop. They don't want to interrupt RAMONA and her FATHER. They eavesdrop.)

RAMONA. Daddy, what's happening to our family? Aunt Bea is going to Alaska—you're feeling sad all day 'cause of money and jobs— and Mom works so hard she's tired and grumpy a lot. Beezus won't even hug me. *(MRS. QUIMBY and BEEZUS enter the room and the conversation energetically.)*

MRS. QUIMBY. Ramona, I don't need to hear this after a long day. I have a headache, and I'm starving.

BEEZUS. This is gonna be another of those family scenes, all about Ramona and her feelings. Try being the oldest sometimes, and everybody thinks you're already grown up so they can ignore you but you're really not and you get stuck all the time taking care of your little sister, and nobody listens to you.

MR. QUIMBY. Beezus, please.

BEEZUS. Ramona needs to grow up.

RAMONA. Can't you see I'm trying?

BEEZUS. Try harder. Daddy, you smoked.

MRS. QUIMBY. Bob, you didn't...

MR. QUIMBY. One stale cigarette, Dorie. That was it. Beezus, I'm not perfect, and neither is anybody in this family. *(He stands, and shouts.)* ATTENTION, ALL QUIMBYS! *(Everybody quiets, listens.)* We have to stop this grumping around. I have decided that we are going out to dinner. We are going to the Whopperburger, and we are all going to smile, and be pleasant to each other if it kills us. That's an order.

RAMONA. The Whopperburger?

MR. QUIMBY. Why not? The sky's the limit?

MRS. QUIMBY. Bob, are you sure we can...

MR. QUIMBY. This family *needs* a break.

WHOPPERBURGER HOSTESS VOICE OVER *(on mic).* Quimby, party of four! Quimby, party of four! *(The Quimby living room and Klickitat Street are gone.)*

SCENE TWENTY-FIVE

(The Whopperburger is all around them. It's a glorious hamburger restaurant, full of lights and giant hamburger decor. As the QUIMBYS enter, the two troops of SCOUTS, boy and girl, all wearing Whopperburger giveaway hats, exit with their usual precision and panache.

Two tables are visible. At the smaller one the OLD MAN with a straw hat, who we've seen walking many times on Klickitat Street, sits alone. His food is in front of him, and he has his napkin tucked under his chin. The other table is large, and empty. The QUIMBYS are heading toward it. As they pass the OLD MAN on the way, he catches RAMONA's eye.)

OLD MAN *(tipping his hat to RAMONA).* Well, young lady! Have you been good to your mother? *(RAMONA is too shy to answer, but she gives the man a little smile. He responds with a salute. RAMONA goes on to the Quimby table.)*

BEEZUS. Ramona, why didn't you answer that man?

RAMONA. I'm not supposed to talk to strangers.

BEEZUS. But Mom and Dad are with us. That rule's for when you're alone.

(The WAITRESS arrives, rapidly.)

WAITRESS. Hi, I'm Tammy! Sorry I'm late. I had a bazillion clean-ups to do back there. First, your Whoppersong. *(She sings to the table.)*

> Forget your pots, forget your pans
> It's not too late to change your plans
> Spend a little...

MR. QUIMBY. We'll skip the song today, if you don't mind. We're pretty hungry. *(The WAITRESS begins to talk very quickly, and faster as she goes on.)*

WAITRESS. "Don't get nervous, speedy service!" That's our Whoppermotto, and that's what Whopperburger's all about. What'll it be, folks? *(The QUIMBYS pick up her rhythm, and so the following sequence happens fast.)*

MRS. QUIMBY. Cheesewhopper. Coke.

WAITRESS. Cheesewhopper! Coke.

MR. QUIMBY. Chiliwhopper. Coke.

WAITRESS. Chiliwhopper! Coke.

BEEZUS. Veggiewhopper. Coke.

WAITRESS. Veggiewhopper! Coke.

RAMONA. Doublewhopper, fries, and a chocolate shake.

WAITRESS. Doublewhopper, fries, and a chocolate shake!
(The WAITRESS zooms off to the kitchen. A moment of silence at the Quimby table. The OLD MAN waves and grins at RAMONA, after catching her eye. RAMONA doesn't know what to do. She shyly waves back.)

MRS. QUIMBY. I want to say, to the whole family, that we've all...

(WAITRESS returns with their food, spins the dishes onto the table with inconceivable rapidity, each burger [and BEEZUS' Veggiewhopper, which might look like a huge carrot on a bun] landing right in front of its recipient.)

WAITRESS *(as she lays the platters down)*. Here we are, folks! Cheesewhopper, Coke! Chiliwhopper, Coke! Veggiewhopper, Coke! Doublewhopper, fries, and a chocolate shake! Enjoy! *(The WAITRESS zooms off.)*

MRS. QUIMBY. I was saying we've all been trying our best to keep this family together, and you girls have both been terrific. I'm sorry if I've been too worried and too busy lately. I know there hasn't been enough love to go around our house.

RAMONA. There's been enough for Beezus. 'Cause she's older, and doesn't whine, and never gets in trouble at school, and...

MR. QUIMBY. Ramona, you and Beezus *are* very different kids. That doesn't mean we can't love you both.

MRS. QUIMBY. Loving Beezus doesn't mean we don't have enough love left for you. Love isn't a cup of sugar that gets used up. *(MRS. QUIMBY hugs RAMONA.)*

MR. QUIMBY. Your mom's right, little sparkler. There's plenty of love to go around. *(The QUIMBYS sit solemnly for a moment.)*

BEEZUS. Let's eat! I'm starving! *(ALL dive into their burgers, and chomp away. The OLD MAN, having finished his dinner, gets up from his table. He glances over at the QUIMBYS eating, and leaves the restaurant.)*

MR. QUIMBY. Listen, everybody. I've been feeling sorry for myself long enough. I've got a feeling my luck is about to change, and I'm going to help it along. Whatever it takes. Here goes...I'm stopping smoking *now*. Not for a week, but forever.

BEEZUS *(standing, raising her glass).* A toast to our non-smoking dad—and all the Quimbys! *(All QUIMBYS stand and raise their glasses high: three Cokes and a chocolate shake.)*

RAMONA. Hooray for us!

(They drink. They cheer, very loudly. Their WAITRESS appears.)

MR. QUIMBY. Tammy! Check, please.

WAITRESS. It's your lucky night. Your meals have been paid for.

MRS. QUIMBY. Paid for? By whom?

WAITRESS. The man who was sitting at that table.

MRS. QUIMBY. But we don't even know him.

WAITRESS. Maybe he knows you.

BEEZUS. Why would he pay for our dinners?

WAITRESS. "Because," he said, "they are a very loving family, and because I miss my wife, and children, and my grandchildren very much." *(RAMONA leaps up from the table, runs toward the door of the restaurant and the street.)*

MR. QUIMBY. RAMONA! Where are you going?

MRS. QUIMBY. RAMONA!

BEEZUS. Let her go. *(RAMONA reaches the street, downstage. She looks in every direction for the OLD MAN, wanting to comfort him, to thank him. He is in the distance, about to disappear into the night when he sees RAMONA, stops. He salutes, and RAMONA salutes in return. He is gone. The rest of the QUIMBYS exit the Whopperburger, come downstage to join RAMONA.)*

RAMONA. He's gone.

MRS. QUIMBY. You know, I think that man was right. We are a loving family.

RAMONA. Not all the time.

MR. QUIMBY. Nobody is loving and sweet *all* the time. If they are, they're boring.

BEEZUS. We are a lot nicer than some families I know. Some families don't even eat dinner together...

MRS. QUIMBY. Or laugh together.

BEEZUS. That man paying for our dinners was sort of like a happy ending.

RAMONA. A happy ending...for today. *(Lights dim, and out, except for a light on BEEZUS, in narrator mode.)*

SCENE TWENTY-SIX

(Ramona's bedroom slowly appears in another area behind BEEZUS. RAMONA is in bed.)

BEEZUS. The truth is, in spite of the fights, I like my sister Ramona better all the time. She still drives me crazy, but she's really growing up. She helped my dad a lot with his smoking, and she even learned to handle old Griggs near the end of the third grade...*(RAMONA gets out of bed in her nightgown.)*

RAMONA. Beezus? I can't sleep.

BEEZUS. Me neither.

RAMONA. I keep thinking about Aunt Bea.

(In the distance, Bea's window in her apartment building lights up. She's dancing by herself to some melancholy music. She stops, and drapes a white scarf over her head and shoulders like a wedding shawl.)

BEEZUS. That she's leaving poor you?

RAMONA. It's not that. She really wants a wedding, with flowers and everything. I know she does.

BEEZUS. I think you're right, Ramona. But you heard them. There's no time to do it all, and they're leaving the day after tomorrow.

RAMONA. Mom and Dad had a wedding. Aunt Bea should have one too.

BEEZUS. Maybe if Hobart knew how much Aunt Bea wanted one...

RAMONA. Maybe there's some kind of special super-fast wedding he can make...*(With decision.)* Tomorrow morning, I'm going to tell Mr. Hobart Kemp to *do* it.

BEEZUS. He's a grown-up, Ramona. You can't boss him around.

RAMONA. Maybe he'll think it's a good idea, especially if you come too, and we *both* tell him...*(Lights fade on the GIRLS as they confer, whispering to each other about their plans. BEA looks out her window toward Klickitat Street, and her light clicks out.)*

SCENE TWENTY-SEVEN

(Morning, the following day on Klickitat Street. It's summertime. Fans, lawn sprinklers, etc. HOBART, RAMONA, BEEZUS and HOWIE rush on. HOBART is dragging HOWIE under protest. MR. and MRS. QUIMBY come out to greet them.)

HOBART. Howie, it's not gonna kill ya...

MR. QUIMBY. Hobart!

MRS. QUIMBY. And Howie! It's so nice to...

HOBART. No time for chit-chat. Bob...Dorothy...It's gonna be the fastest wedding in the west. And the most beautiful!

MRS. QUIMBY. Wedding?

MR. QUIMBY. I thought you and Bea were leaving for Alaska tomorrow.

HOBART. We are. But these daughters of yours convinced me. Bea feels she'll be missing something wonderful—and she'll never have the chance again. I'm persuaded. The wedding's on.

MRS. QUIMBY. But the dresses, the flowers, the invitations...

MR. QUIMBY. By tomorrow? Impossible.

HOBART. By *this afternoon.* No problem!

MRS. QUIMBY. Just where is this wedding going to be?

HOBART. Rose City Presbyterian! I called Pastor Jones and he had to cancel a fishing trip, so we're in luck!

MR. QUIMBY. Who's the best man?

HOBART. Howie. I've captured him already. And the two maids of honor are right here.

BEEZUS. Mom, you've still got your wedding dress in a trunk upstairs. That would fit Aunt Bea.

MRS. QUIMBY. Yes, but...

HOBART. Dorothy, your job is to get the bride into that dress by three o'clock. Bob, invite the neighborhood!

MR. QUIMBY. No problem!

HOBART. We've got shopping to do. Where do they sell bride and groom stuff?

BEEZUS. I think there's a wedding shop in the mall. They should...

HOBART. Let's go! (*HOWIE pulls his hand out of HOBART's, runs a few feet away.*) Howie...?

HOWIE. I wanted to ride my bike today. Besides, I don't like weddings. I went to one once and threw up.

RAMONA. Come on, Howie. Be grown-up. You'll look terrific in a best man suit. And we'll ride bikes right after. Please.

HOWIE. Awwwwwwww...okay.

HOBART. Ramona Quimby, I'm going to fly you, and Beezus, to Alaska at your very first school vacation, so you can see your Aunt Bea, and ride on a moose.

RAMONA (*still slightly suspicious of HOBART*). For real?

HOBART. All for real, Ramona. And I'd like it if you'd start calling me Uncle Hobart a little early.

RAMONA. Okay, Uncle Hobart. Let's go! Howie!

SCENE TWENTY-EIGHT

(Selma's Bridal Shoppe, all white dresses, lace, and tuxedos. It features a SELMA'S BRIDAL SHOPPE sign, and a huge three-way mirror. SELMA is in the shop. She faces HOBART, HOWIE, RAMONA and BEEZUS with some distaste. They're a mess, and she's extremely proper. Her hair is amazingly overdone.)

SELMA. No garden supplies, jeans, or skateboards. This is a *bridal* shop. Fine wedding wear for ladies and gentlemen.

HOBART. Selma?

SELMA. Yes?

HOBART. Are you ready for the ultimate bridal shop challenge?

SELMA. I'm ready to call the police.

HOBART. What do they know about weddings? One groom outfit for me, one best man for Howie. I hear that pink and black is coming back.

SELMA. Not in this shop it isn't.

HOBART. Black suits, black shoes, pink bow ties and pink cummerbunds. For the ladies, two beautiful maid of honor dresses. Ramona, what color for you?

RAMONA. Pink, with pink Mary Janes.

BEEZUS. Same for me, only I want heels.

HOBART. 'Atta girl.

SELMA. When do you need these by?

HOBART. That's the challenge. This afternoon.

SELMA. This afternoon!?

HOBART. Yep.

SELMA. Impossible. *(Silence. HOBART is the picture of dejection. HOWIE looks relieved. RAMONA and BEEZUS start to cry, hanging onto each other. It's a good act, be-*

cause they mean it. They only exaggerate a little.) Don't!
Oh, please don't...Don't cry girls. I hate crying, except at
weddings. Please...(RAMONA and BEEZUS sob more
loudly. SELMA is moved, and suddenly decisive.) On second thought, girls, nothing is impossible at Selma's! Stop
crying, please! The fitting rooms are right this way.

HOWIE. Oh oh!

HOBART. Howard! (RAMONA and BEEZUS stop crying immediately, grin at each other and HOBART. RAMONA,
BEEZUS, and HOWIE enter the bridal shop unit, do a
quick change.) Selma, we'll need flowers! One bridal bouquet, two bridesmaid bouquets, two boutonnieres for
groom and best man, and flowers for everywhere. Lots of
them.

SELMA. What color?

HOBART (shouting to the KIDS). What color?

RAMONA, HOWIE, BEEZUS (offstage). Pink!

HOBART. Pink. (HOBART slaps a stack of money into SEL-
MA's palm, clearly more than she expected. She's pleased.
HOBART runs off.)

SELMA. Pink is coming back. (She exits counting her
money.)

(RAMONA comes out looking very grown up and beautiful
in her dress. RAMONA goes to the three-way mirror to
look at her new self.)

RAMONA. Is that me? That very grown-up maid of honor?
It's me! (Music begins. Three other Ramonas look back at
her. She smiles. They smile. She raises her arm. They raise
an arm and start copying everything she does.) Three of
me! Beautiful, glorious me! (And then, three other Ramonas appear behind them...and three more...and on...and

*on... down to some small Ramona puppets way off in the
distance. Hundreds of Ramonas. RAMONA FOREVER.)* I
go on forever. *(She raises an arm. They all do. She leaps.
They all do. She twirls. They all do.)* Forever me. *(Dance
of the Ramonas. Pure joy in being happy and alive! Unison, but sometimes the mirror figures break unison and different Ramonas, or groups of Ramonas, do different moves.
We return to mirror unison in the end. End dance. End
music. All Ramonas but the original are gone. BEEZUS is
there in her dress, along with HOWIE in his suit, and HO-
BART, resplendent in a pink and black wedding tuxedo.
HOWIE, BEEZUS and RAMONA take their positions, a bit
off to one side. HOBART stands, as a groom should, before
the MINISTER, waiting for his bride. Music, the "Wedding
March," simple and soft.)*

*(BEA emerges in her wedding gown. She looks beautiful.
GUESTS assemble. Pink flowers rain from above. As she
solemnly walks toward her place at HOBART's side...)*

staggered on SR

SCENE TWENTY-NINE

HOWIE *(singing just loud enough for us to hear).*
     Here comes the bride, big, fat and wide
     Here comes the groom, skinny as a broom...

RAMONA. Howie, keep quiet! *(BEA stands beside HOBART
     before the MINISTER. Music out.)*

MINISTER. I now pronounce you husband and wife. You
     may kiss the bride. *(HOBART and BEA kiss.)*

BEEZUS. Oooooohh!

EVERYONE. CHEERS AND APPLAUSE!!!!! *(BEA tosses her bouquet into the audience. The WEDDING PARTY freezes—HOBART and BEA kissing, others cheering, MR. and MRS. QUIMBY looking on with joy. Lights slowly fade on the wedding. It's gone.)*

leave quickly USR

SCENE THIRTY

(BEEZUS and RAMONA come downstage. Their wedding clothes are gone, and they are dressed for the first day of school. For RAMONA, it's fourth grade! It's autumn on Klickitat Street, and a few yellow leaves are on the ground.)

BEEZUS. Aunt Bea had a *beautiful* wedding.

RAMONA. Nobody spilled punch, *and* nobody threw up.

BEEZUS. We got a postcard from her the other day. She invited us to come up and see her and our new uncle in Alaska whenever we had time off from school.

RAMONA. The card's taped to my bed. It has a picture of a moose walking down the street.

(MRS. QUIMBY appears near their house, dressed for work.)

MRS. QUIMBY. Ramona! Do you have something for Show and Tell?

RAMONA. There's no Show and Tell in *fourth grade*, Mom. That's for babies!

MRS. QUIMBY. Just checking. Have a great first day, both of you. See you when I get home from work. *(She's gone.)*

(MR. QUIMBY appears, dressed for work, walking rapidly.)

MR. QUIMBY. I'm late, girls. Have a great first one, Beezus! Knock 'em out, Ramona! *(He's gone.)*

BEEZUS. You guessed it. My dad got a job.

RAMONA. Finally.

BEEZUS. It's not the kind of job he really wanted. It's at the same frozen food warehouse, back working for Mr. Frost… but he doesn't go back there in the cold part anymore. He's the assistant manager. You know, being grown-up is hard work.

RAMONA. Being a kid and trying to become grown-up is even harder.

BEEZUS. The family budget is still tight. Mom has to keep working, but that's okay 'cause she really likes her job at the doctor's. My dad would love to go back to school and study to be a teacher, and maybe he will someday. But, as I've heard a lot of grown-ups say, we can't always do what we want in life, so we do what we can.

RAMONA. I'm gonna do just exactly what I want in my entire life.

BEEZUS. If you do that, Ramona, you'll be a luckier person than Mom and Dad. You'll be like Aunt Bea and Uncle Hobart, maybe.

RAMONA. I don't want to be like Uncle Hobart, or even Aunt Bea. I want to be like me.

(HOWIE appears from his house next door, ready for the first day of fourth grade. He calls out to RAMONA.)

HOWIE. Come on, Ramona! I want to get there early.

RAMONA. So we can tease the third graders.

RAMONA and HOWIE. Third-grade baby!

HOWIE. Race you to the school yard!

RAMONA. Howie, wait! I want to hear Beezus talk to the audience. *(HOWIE waits impatiently with RAMONA.)*

BEEZUS *(to audience)*. Well...that's a little bit of how we live here. My mom, Dad, Aunt Bea, Uncle Hobart, some friends, and of course, my wonderful sister Ramona.

I'm almost a teen-ager. I know I'll leave here someday and go off to college, Los Angeles, Paris, or someplace. Times change, people change, and everyone grows older...but Klickitat seems to go on forever. There's a new street light sometimes, and the headlines on the newspapers that land on the people's doorsteps always change...but the street stays the same. Let me tell you something interesting. People live here, and sometimes they're happy, and sometimes sad, with all their small everyday adventures—and their life goes on—in a kind of miraculous way.

You know, in the autumn, Klickitat Street is covered with leaves. You should see it. It's beautiful. I think it might be the most beautiful street in the world.

I gotta get to school now. 'Bye, Ramona. 'Bye, Howie. Have a great first day. *(Back out to audience.)* 'Bye, everyone. *(She walks offstage. HOWIE and RAMONA remain.)*

HOWIE. Race you to the school yard! *(He runs off toward Glenwood School. He's gone.)*

RAMONA *(runs after him, calling)*. Howie! Wait for me! *(But the moment before she'd have raced off the stage, she stops, turns to audience.)* 'Bye 'bye! *(RAMONA QUIMBY runs off. Klickitat Street is empty. An autumn leaf falls in the light, and another...)*

END OF PLAY

DIRECTOR'S NOTES

DIRECTOR'S NOTES

DIRECTOR'S NOTES

DIRECTOR'S NOTES

DIRECTOR'S NOTES